UNDERSTANDING IMMIGRATION

One Country to Another

Iris Teichmann

Smart Apple Media

First published in 2005 by Franklin Watts
96 Leonard Street, London EC2A 4XD

Franklin Watts Australia
Level 17/207 Kent Street
Sydney NSW 2000

Series editor: Rachel Cooke
Series design: Simon Borrough
Picture research: Diana Morris

Published in the United States by Smart Apple Media
2140 Howard Drive West, North Mankato, Minnesota 56003

Library of Congress Cataloging-in-Publication Data

Teichmann, Iris.
One country to another / by Iris Teichmann.
p. cm. — (Understanding immigration)
Includes index.
ISBN-13 : 978-1-58340-967-1
1. Emigration and immigration—Juvenile literature. 2. Immigrants—Juvenile literature. I. Title.

JV6201.T44 2006
304.8'2—dc22   2005051731

9 8 7 6 5 4 3 2 1

Acknowledgements: The author and publishers would like to thank all those people who were interviewed for this book. In addition, we would also like to acknowledge the following sources: Migration statistics, p.9, International Organization for Migration (IMO). William Bradford's journal, p.11, Pilgrim Hall Museum, Plymouth, MA. Anna Tuniks's story, p.12, *Kennebec Journal*, 5/11/1968. Danko Joszef's story, p.13, Katharine Knox and Tony Kushner, *Refugees in an Age of Genocide*, Frank Cass, 1999. Mahmut Aktaz's story, p.15, David Bacon, *Germany's New Identity—A Nation of Immigrants*. Statistics, p.16, Oranization for Migration. A Kurd's story, p.17, British Refugee Council. Irena's story, p.19, Deborah Barndt, University of York, Ontario. Dr. 'Yele Aluko's story, p.23, interview by Tina Puryear. Lydia's story, p.24, Anti-Slavery International. Mrs. Murphy's story, p.26, interview conducted by Elizabeth M. Buckingham on behalf of the U.S. Works Project Administration on December 4, 1939, Connecticut State Library. Nurul's story, p.27, World Bank. Kurt's story, p.28, United States Holocaust Memorial Museum, Washington, D.C. Beatrice's story, p.30, Amnesty International. Gulcan's story, p.31, Expatica Netherlands. Sa Myint Swe's and Nan Khin Win's story, p.33, Sanctuary Refugee Foundation, New South Wales, Australia. Basi's story, p.34, British Refugee Council. A tragic story, p.35, Houston Chronicle 5/18/2003. The Pearse family's story, p.37, Napier City Council, New Zealand. A Tamil's story, p.38, British Refugee Council. Magdalena's story, p.39, Pilar Marrero, Pacific News Service. Aneta's story, p.40, Izabela Grabowska, Center of Migration Research, University of Warsaw. Migration statistics, p.41, International Organization for Migration.

Contents

Migrants and immigrants

Who's who

We live in a world where more and more people are moving from one country to another. Experts estimate that there are around 150 million people who work outside their country of birth. They are migrants. Most usually stay for a few months or a few years before they return home or move on to another country. But migrants become immigrants if they decide to make the country they work in their permanent home.

Push factors

People usually decide to move to another country because of bad situations or events at home. Such situations or events are called push factors. For example, most people leave because they cannot survive or make enough money in their own country. Other push factors include natural disasters, wars, unstable governments, and a lack of human rights.

In 1992, war in Bosnia forced many people to flee the country and become refugees.

Pull factors

There are also things that attract people to other countries—these are called pull factors. People may, for example, have hopes of earning more money. They may look forward to a higher standard of living, a more promising career for themselves, and a better education for their children. Or they may simply want to live in a country where they have freedom and security.

Global impact

Only a small proportion of the world's population actually become migrants, but their movement can have a big impact. Countries from which people leave—so-called sending countries—can lose valuable workers with skills and expertise. But they can also benefit when migrants send money back home to family members. Receiving countries—the ones to which people move—can benefit because employers have a larger pool of available workers, which in turn benefits the countries' economies.

On arrival in another country, migrants need to present passports and usually visas to the authorities.

AS A MATTER OF FACT

According to migration experts, the number of people living in another country for more than a year has increased steadily since the 1970s. In 1965, for example, around 75 million people lived abroad. By 1990, this number had risen to about 120 million. But these figures still represent only a small amount of the world's population. Today, less than three percent of people live away from home for a year or more.

Immigration in the past

THE NORMAN STORY:
SPREADING NORMAN CULTURE

In 1066, William the Conqueror invaded England and moved his court from Normandy in France to London. Although comparatively few in number, the Norman immigrants ruthlessly took complete control of the country. From their position of power, they had a huge influence on England's language, law, customs, and architecture.

Pembroke Castle was one of many built by the Normans in England and Wales to show their authority over the people they had conquered.

Early migration

People have moved from one place to another for a very long time. Experts think that around 30,000 years ago, humans arrived in North America by crossing an ice-age land bridge between Siberia and Alaska. Until about 10,000 years ago, people lived a nomadic life as hunter-gatherers, moving from one area to another in search of food and shelter.

Farms, trade, and war

Farming, and a more settled lifestyle, began when people started breeding animals and selecting plants to grow. But people continued to move. They farmed new areas of land and began trading with other groups of people. They also built towns and cities, to which more people moved. Invasions and wars were other reasons why people moved. Invasions could force people to leave their homes. They also brought immigrants and their culture from the invading country, as happened when the Normans conquered England.

Exploring and migrating

As trade and technology developed in Europe in the late 1400s and the 1500s, the great age of exploration began. Europeans started exploring Africa, North and South America, and Asia. They set up farms and businesses overseas. In the early 1600s, the first English settlers to move to North America were the Pilgrims. Gradually, more Europeans moved abroad not only to improve their livelihoods, but also to enjoy political and religious freedom. At the same time, another form of migrants came to the New World—those forced from Africa as slaves. All of these forms of migration affected the developing culture of America.

An artist's depiction of the Pilgrims embarking for the New World.

THE PILGRIMS' STORY: EARLY SETTLERS

The Pilgrims were strict Christians who broke away from the Church of England. In 1620, the first Pilgrims left England for North America, on board the ship the *Mayflower*, in search of religious freedom. This is what William Bradford, one of the first Pilgrims, wrote about his companions when they arrived in North America:

"They fell upon their knees and blessed ye God of heaven, who had brought them over ye vast and furious ocean, and delivered them from all ye periles and miseries thereof, againe to set their feete on ye firme and stable earth, their proper elemente."

Slaves were brought from Africa to America and forced to work for the new colonies.

Immigrants to the U.S. in the late 19th and early 20th century found work in America's burgeoning factories. These workers are assembling the new Model T Ford in 1915.

Mass movements

In the 19th and early 20th century, millions of Europeans left their homes for North and South America, South Africa, Australia, and Asia. Between the 1840s and the 1920s, the United States alone saw the arrival of around 37 million immigrants from Germany, Ireland, Italy, Britain, and the Scandinavian countries. A few left hoping for adventure, but the vast majority wanted to escape poverty and unemployment back home.

Escaping wars

The period also saw a huge movement of refugees—people fleeing political turmoil and war. World War II resulted in more than 50 million refugees moving from one place to another within Europe. Some ended up in the U.S.

ANNA TUNIKS'S STORY: FROM RUSSIA TO AMERICA

Anna Tuniks was a Russian Orthodox immigrant who, after a long journey, settled in Richmond, Maine, in the 1950s. This is what she wrote in a letter to a local newspaper in May 1968:

"There are so many of us 'old Russians' who didn't choose Richmond, Maine.... We came here to live and to build. Some of us lost hundreds of acres of land, estates, and mansions, converted to museums after the Revolution in Russia. In Europe, we toiled, saved, built, and lost again. Now, in the '50s, we considered ourselves fortunate to become part of this country. This time we were ready to build again, true...on a smaller scale, with less strength and with a quaint accent in English."

Going West

World War II left many countries in central and eastern Europe in ruins. People could not find work and also suffered from the lack of political freedom imposed by the communist Soviet Union, which controlled the eastern half of Europe.

In the 1950s and 1960s, many people fled to western Europe. Danko Joszef was one of the 150,000 people from Hungary and Poland who were allowed into Britain.

In November 1956, Soviet troops brutally supressed an uprising in Hungary. Thousands of Hungarians like Danko fled to western Europe.

DANKO JOSZEF'S STORY: MINING IMMIGRANT

On New Year's Eve 1956, 16-year-old Danko Joszef left Hungary for Graz, Austria. There he saw a notice advertising jobs working in coal mines in Britain.

"So I handed my papers in, and it came to New Year's Day and they put us on the train the following day to England. On the third, I was in Scotland in Stirling coal mine.... I was rather fortunate, I suppose, because I didn't want to stay in a refugee camp, because the longer you stay there, the harder it becomes to settle."

13

Immigration today

Global migration

Immigration continues today, but unlike in the past when Europeans left to live abroad, Europe itself has seen a steady stream of migrants and immigrants in recent decades. At the same time, countries whose history is largely built on the arrival of immigrants—such as the U.S., Canada, and Australia—continue to receive people from other countries, both temporarily and permanently.

A crowd watches a street entertainer. Most Western cities today are home to people from all over the world.

Modern immigrants

Most of the people on the move come from developing countries. One reason is that travel has become easier and cheaper. But the main reason is the changes that have taken place in these countries, many of which are still struggling politically and economically after gaining independence from foreign rule. Many people in Africa, Asia, and Latin America therefore leave. Most go to neighboring countries, but some go to Australasia, North America, and Europe.

14

Immigration control

The arrival of many migrants from different cultural and ethnic backgrounds has become a challenge for governments in developed countries because of resentment among the local population. Many people consider newcomers to be a threat to their economy and way of life. In response, governments have established strict immigration laws to control who is allowed to live and work in their countries. However, in some instances, migration has become easier. For example, the European Union (EU) allows people from any of its member states to live and work, more or less freely, in any other country within the Union.

Working and settling

Immigration laws can allow people to live and work temporarily in a country. They can also allow people to apply to settle in a country. Many people who decide to settle in another country want to join family members who are already living there. Their relatives often came in the past because of special recruitment programs. In the 1950s, for example, Germany recruited thousands of Turkish guest workers to work in factories.

MAHMUT AKTAZ'S STORY: HIS FATHER'S EXPERIENCE

In 1980, Mahmut Aktaz went to live in Germany with his mother and family. His father had arrived as a guest worker in 1963. Aktaz recalls his father's descriptions of Germany:

"He was all alone back then. He said Germany was a green country, with big factories, wide boulevards, and large cities. But they didn't accept him there. He didn't have his family with him, and he didn't speak the language well."

Today, Mahmut works in a major car manufacturing plant in Germany.

Hungarians celebrate joining the European Union in May 2004. Twenty-five states are now members of the organization, working toward common political and economic goals.

15

Less than 1%

1% to 10%

10.1% to 20%

More than 20%

This map shows the number of migrants in a country as a percentage of its total population.

AS A MATTER OF FACT

The U.S. and Russia have the biggest numbers of migrants from abroad, with around 35 million and 13.3 million foreigners living and working there respectively. Other top countries with large numbers of migrants are Germany (7.3 million), Ukraine (6.9 million), France (6.3 million), India (6.3 million), Canada (5.8 million), Saudi Arabia (5.3 million), and Australia (4.7 million). Britain comes in much lower on the list, with 4 million migrants.

Labor migration

In the past, most people migrated not just to find work but to build a new life. Today, the majority of migrants do not intend to settle in their new country. There are two main reasons why. First, many people only get permission to work abroad for a certain period of time. Second, because most migrants come from developing countries, they often go abroad to work and save money and then return home to benefit from their countries' developing economies.

Legal migration

Most developed countries allow people with special skills or expertise to apply for permission to come and work. Such people include entrepreneurs setting up new businesses abroad, teachers, doctors and nurses, and technology specialists. People with little or no skills can often apply to work in developed countries as well—usually in industries for which there are not enough local workers, such as farming, catering, construction, or manufacturing.

A KURD'S STORY: BEING SMUGGLED

A Kurdish Iranian woman who did not want to reveal her name describes how she got to England with the help of a smuggler:

"The smuggler took my passport and gave me a different one. According to the deal, I paid $500 in advance and then another $500.... He [also] took my watch and told me not to talk to anyone before I departed [from Istanbul airport]."

The woman and her daughter also had to pay for the journey from Iran to Turkey. Both ended up on a flight to London's Heathrow Airport after a month's wait.

Illegal migration

But work programs for people with few skills are limited, and not every developed country has them. Many migrants, therefore, work in other countries illegally. Traveling illegally often means relying on smugglers to arrange the journey and false identity documents, such as passports. This can be very expensive: some migrants pay smugglers as much as $20,000 to arrange their passage to Europe or North America.

These illegal migrants have been discovered trying to cross a border hidden in a truck.

Leaving poverty behind

Basic existence

Most migrants from developing countries leave in search of better-paying jobs. The majority of people in developing countries earn a basic living from farming or making and selling things. These jobs often belong to the so-called informal economy, in which people neither pay taxes nor have any protection against exploitative bosses. People living on incomes from activities in the informal economy can make enough money to survive, but rarely enough to improve their lives.

In Kenya, many people find work on large-scale farms producing cash crops, such as roses, to sell to the developed world.

The global market

Today, the biggest buyers of farm products from developing countries are the supermarkets of the developed world. But small-scale farmers are unable to produce the amount of food supermarkets want at the low prices they demand, so small-scale farmers often find it difficult to survive. Some farmers may find jobs with much bigger farms that provide supermarkets with products.

AS A MATTER OF FACT

Farm work is usually hard and poorly paid. Large-scale farmers in developed countries depend heavily on foreign migrant workers who are willing to work very hard in return for more money than they could make at home. In Britain, there are an estimated 90,000 eastern European migrants working on farms.

Moving away

Other small-scale farmers may leave the countryside to find work in cities. There is an increasing number of industries in the cities of many developing countries, but there is also an increasing number of people moving from the countryside—which means that there are often not enough jobs to go around. Migration to another country is the next step for many people, such as Irena.

Harvesting tomatoes. Farmers always require extra workers at harvest time.

IRENA'S STORY: SEASONAL WORKER

Irena lives in Miacatlan in Mexico. Every year she leaves her family behind and travels to Canada to pick tomatoes for four months.

"I cleared $1,000 in two weeks," she told an interviewer. This is almost a year's salary for a Mexican farm worker. The money means that Irena's family can gradually improve their standard of living and afford luxury items such as a television and a washer.

Social status

Many people in countries such as China are no longer satisfied with earning just enough to survive. They want to improve their standard of living to match that of people in the developed world, and to improve their social status. To be able to do this, many go abroad and send the money they earn back to their families.

Helping back home

Today, many parents in China put immense pressure on their children to find work abroad. In some areas, virtually all people of working age have migrated. Having children working abroad is a source of pride for most Chinese parents. The money the children send home benefits the local economy, too. Since the 1990s, money sent back by people like Gao Jinquan has helped his village in southern China. Families have built new houses and spent more money on local businesses.

GAO JINQUAN'S STORY: NO CHOICE BUT TO LEAVE

Gao Jinquan was 17 when he left China to find work in the West. There were no job prospects for him at home, and all of his friends were leaving, too. Like many Chinese immigrants in the West, Gao Jinquan worked in Chinese restaurants. But because he knew some of the local language, he worked as a waiter instead of in the kitchens. He is now married and has a child.

"I would have liked to go to college, but competition for jobs is very tough. I came with two friends from my village. So many other people from my village have gone abroad to work and support their families in China. Our village has become very prosperous."

A Chinese restaurant in New York. Restaurant work is often the first option for immigrants.

Staying

While most migrants intend to go back home after they have saved up enough money, many stay in their new country. Some stay because the government allows them to remain as permanent immigrants. Others stay because they have adapted to the lifestyle of their new country, or because they have married a local person. Others have built a career for themselves in their new home and have been able to bring their families over.

BASARIELLO'S STORY: FINDING WORK

Basariello comes from a poor family in Naples, Italy. As a young man without much education or work skills, he made a basic living by working in mines and on building sites.

"In 1962, I was offered a work permit to work in Germany in the building trade. Having gone back to Italy, I then got another job offer in Germany in 1968. I left Italy to find safer and better work. Three of my sons have joined me. One of my sons has gone to Canada. In those days, it was difficult getting work in Italy."

Basariello eventually became a landscape gardener and has worked for the same firm ever since—even now that he's supposedly retired!

A Chinese farm laborer works in a paddy field. Behind her are the modern apartment buildings of her village, financed by money sent home from abroad.

21

A hospital in Tanzania. Frustration with poor facilities and infrastructure cause many doctors in the developing world to look for work outside their own country.

Better prospects

In less developed countries, people with a good education and employment skills often want to go to Europe or North America to find a job in their chosen career. This move gives them the chance to earn more money, gain valuable work experience, and improve their career prospects. Such prospects are often lacking back home, where there may not be enough money, political stability, or a developed infrastructure.

Brain drain

The term "brain drain" is used to describe the loss of skills and expertise a country suffers when many of its well-educated people migrate. Many African countries have been particularly affected by brain drain because they have suffered from war—another reason why people want to leave home. Brain drain can seriously affect a country's ability to develop its industries, as well as its education and health care systems. For example, more than 20,000 Nigerian doctors have gone to work in Canada and the U.S.

DR. 'YELE ALUKO'S STORY: FROM NIGERIA TO THE U.S.

Dr. 'Yele Aluko is from Nigeria, where he studied medicine. After working as a doctor in Nigeria for two years, he wanted to develop his career.

"I went to the U.S. to do post-graduate studies specializing in cardiology. I only intended to stay three or four years. But politics in Nigeria changed. So even though we had excellent training in Nigeria, we couldn't go back and apply it, as the facilities in public hospitals became very poor. Specialists trained in modern practices need electricity and clean running water. We simply couldn't work and use our specialist knowledge."

As Dr. Aluko was sponsored by the hospital he works at, he was able to get a green card and stay in the U.S.

"I am happy now. I miss home, but I believe home is where you make it."

Thinking about home

Educated migrants tend to earn more money and find it easier to learn a new language than less educated migrants—so they often adapt well to a new life abroad. But many continue to feel a strong tie to their home country. Some may even think about returning home to use the experience gained abroad to help build their country. This can be an attractive option if their home country is experiencing rapid economic growth, or if it is recovering from a war.

Many educated migrants first leave their country to study abroad.

Women migrants

Making it alone

Today, more and more women are becoming migrants in their own right. Some join their husbands or relatives already settled abroad and become immigrants. The majority, however, migrate on their own to earn money to send back home to their families. In recent years, women have been able to improve their job prospects, become financially independent, and gain status back home. In Asian countries alone, more women migrate than men.

Working hard

Women migrants tend to have less education than men who go abroad for work. As a result, many women end up working in low-skilled jobs in factories, hotels, and restaurants, and in private homes as domestic workers. While they can earn more money than in their home countries, their working conditions—including very long working hours—are often poor. Many women migrants frequently move from job to job in search of better working conditions and pay.

Domestic workers from the Philippines living in Hong Kong huddle together on their day off.

LYDIA'S STORY: BEING TRAFFICKED

Lydia (not her real name) was 18 when traffickers sent her from the Ukraine to Albania and then to Britain. The traffickers had initially promised to get her to Britain illegally and find her a job, but instead they forced her to work as a prostitute.

"My dream was just to study and get my own place and just get a proper job and get my family; a nice life like everybody else. I've been trafficked twice from Albania since I've arrived in London. And the first time I came to England and they caught me again in the prostitution game and deported me, so the second time the traffickers forced me again to get back to prostitution. But, then, in the end, I tried my best and I had help from people."

Recognizing Lydia's risk of being caught by the traffickers if she returned home, the British government gave her permission to stay for three years—but it is not certain whether she will be able to remain in Britain for good.

This Albanian woman was trafficked to Italy and, like Lydia, forced to work as a prostitute. She did not want her full face to be photographed.

Being exploited

Women in developing countries are often attracted by offers of jobs abroad from local recruitment agencies. Sometimes these job offers are false. The "recruiters"— who are actually criminals called traffickers—send women abroad, take their money and passports away, and force them to work for no money. Many eastern European women in particular have been sent to another country by traffickers and forced to work in the sex industry.

Migrating to survive

Most European immigrants in the 19th and early 20th centuries left their homes in order to survive. Population growth was very rapid at this time, so the competition for food and jobs had become immense. When crops failed—as Ireland's all-important potato crop did between 1845 and 1849—the fight for survival became much harder still. Ireland's potato famine caused the death of around one-third of its population and led millions to journey abroad for work. This mass emigration continued for many years, even after the famine was over, as Ireland struggled to recover from its impact.

A priest blesses a family of Irish emigrants as they leave their home in 1851.

MRS. MURPHY'S STORY:
FROM IRELAND TO AMERICA

Mrs. Murphy was born in Kerry in Ireland in 1864. Taxes imposed by the British government had a heavy impact on her father's farming business, so the family arranged for her to travel to the U.S. on her own.

"I left my homeland to make my way in a new world, very heavy at heart. I had a married aunt in Bridgeport [Connecticut], so I made this city my destination. About three weeks after my arrival, my aunt obtained a position for me in a Yankee family.... I was very blue [unhappy] in America."

NURUL'S STORY: FROM COUNTRY TO CITY

Nurul Islam is a poor man in his late 30s from Ulipur Thana, Bangladesh. He struggles to maintain his household of five, which includes his elderly mother and a divorced sister. In the course of a year, Nurul works as a day laborer during the six-month peak agricultural season. For the other six months, he migrates to Dhaka, the capital city. There he pulls a rickshaw or does any job he can find. Nurul does not see his life changing. He says he can only hope to earn enough to provide sufficient food for his household.

Poverty trap

Today, the poorest people are the least likely to migrate abroad. People suffering severe hardship—because their country has economic problems or because it is hit by famine or other natural disasters—tend to move to other parts of the same country or, if necessary, to neighboring countries. They lack the money to travel to countries on other continents and may not have access to information about opportunities abroad.

Fleeing disasters

Natural disasters such as floods, storms, or erupting volcanoes can force people to migrate for their survival. These disasters often have a devastating effect on a country's infrastructure and economy, which can make it very hard for people to return once they have left. It is probable that many thousands of people who have lost their livelihood and home in the tsunami disaster of 2004 will migrate to the Middle East in order to find work.

A family stands in a street in Indonesia, devastated by the 2004 tsunami.

Persecution

The other reasons why people are forced to migrate have to do with persecution, political upheaval, and war. People face persecution if they are in some way different from others, either because of their race, religion, culture, or political views. Jewish people have suffered from a very long history of persecution. During the 1930s and 1940s, the Nazis in Germany persecuted and killed millions of Jewish people. Many Jews fled to Australia, Europe, and North America to seek safety.

KURT'S STORY:
ESCAPING NAZI GERMANY

Kurt Klein was born in Waldorf, Germany, in 1920. He left for the U.S. in 1937, but his parents were less fortunate—they were sent to the concentration camp at Auschwitz.

"It was becoming more and more evident that Jews should leave if anybody at all would have them, and not very many countries would.... Since I had relatives in the States, that seemed to be the natural place to go. I was fortunate, and now in retrospect, I know that it must have saved my life."

These young Jewish refugees traveled alone to the U.S. in 1938. They had to leave their parents behind.

Kurdish refugees from Iraq are given medical treatment in a refugee camp in Turkey.

Racial tensions

In today's world, people are still persecuted because of their race. This is because most wars around the world are between different ethnic groups in the same country. In many countries in Asia and Africa, different ethnic groups fight for political power. Once one group becomes dominant, other groups may be in danger of being persecuted—causing people to flee to neighboring countries or even abroad. Kurdish people, for example, have been persecuted in Turkey, Iran, and Iraq, and have been forced to seek refuge in other countries.

Political and religious agitators

At the same time, there are still many people who face persecution for their political or religious beliefs. Some regimes will arrest or even kill citizens who do not practice a certain religion or express political opinions that are seen as a threat to those in power. In many countries, women have fewer rights than men.

ZOE'S STORY: PERSECUTED IN IRAN

Zoe Neirizi actively worked to promote freedom for women and democracy in Iran. She was imprisoned, and her daugther was given to her ex-husband's family. In trouble again after her release, she felt she had no choice but to flee the country.

"It was awful to leave Iran because I had to leave my daughter behind. But it was also very emotional leaving all my memories and belongings and dependencies behind, not knowing when I will go back. When I arrived [in Britain], I hoped to start a new life and build a safe and positive future. I remember that I was also very excited to be free and not to have to look over my shoulders all the time."

Zoe intends to study international law and to work on human rights.

A passenger has his documents checked by an immigration official at a Russian airport.

Seeking asylum

Refugees are people who flee their country because of persecution. When they arrive in another country, many refugees become asylum seekers—they ask the government to recognize them as genuine refugees and allow them to stay. Since the 1980s, the number of people applying for asylum in developed countries has increased. The asylum seekers mostly come from developing countries experiencing conflict or human rights abuses carried out by governments. Most developed countries have established asylum procedures, but in some countries, the system is less formal. Some asylum seekers may simply be sent home.

30

AS A MATTER OF FACT

Asylum seekers have to go through an application process. They gain asylum if the government of their new country recognizes them as refugees as defined by the 1951 United Nations Refugee Convention. This states that refugees are people who are in fear of their lives or freedom because they have a particular nationality, ethnicity, or social standing, or because of their religion or political opinion.

Seeking safety

Some people accuse asylum seekers of coming to a new, richer country so they can live off its welfare, such as unemployment benefits. In fact, the most important things for asylum seekers are safety and access to justice. Most do not choose where to go and instead let smugglers decide the destination. But if they have a relative or even just a named contact in a particular country, they will try to go there.

A Sri Lankan asylum seeker awaits the decision on his refugee status in temporary accommodation provided by a charity.

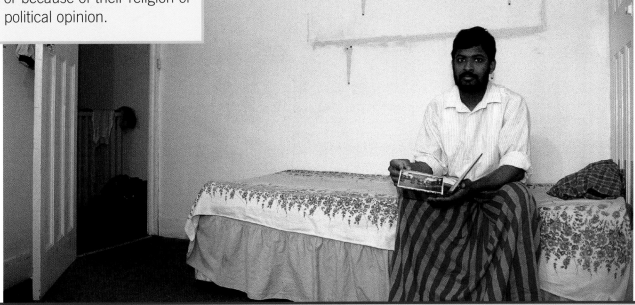

GULCAN'S STORY:
ASYLUM IN THE NETHERLANDS

Gulcan Coban is 37 and lives in Diemen in the Netherlands. Gulcan had to flee Turkey for political reasons. She was arrested by the police for distributing pamphlets while campaigning for workers' rights. She was held in solitary confinement for four years.

"We—myself and the other prisoners—went on a hunger strike in protest against the inhumane conditions. Many people did not survive, and others will suffer the physical effects for life. I was released from prison for several months to allow me to recover, and I fled to the Netherlands. It was the first place I could get to."

Gulcan was given asylum in the Netherlands and was later joined by her son. They have both moved to a new home. Gulcan hopes to teach mathematics, which is what she did back in Turkey.

31

A refugee camp in Chad, which borders on the Darfur region of Sudan. Sudanese people fled to the camp to avoid the conflict in the area.

Refugee camps

When a war breaks out, most people seek immediate safety in a neighboring country. Today, the majority of refugees live in camps in countries bordering their own, where they wait to be able to return home. But this can take years. There are currently millions of refugees living very basic and insecure lives in refugee camps. Many have been there for a long time and may have to remain for longer still.

Resettlement programs

For years, traditional immigration countries such as Australia, Canada, and the U.S. have been operating resettlement programs. The programs identify particularly vulnerable people in refugee camps in Asia, Africa, and South America and allow them to immigrate and build new lives. To qualify for a resettlement program, refugees have to register with United Nations staff and go through a formal interview and assessment procedure. Not all refugees are successful with their application to be resettled.

AS A MATTER OF FACT

There are an estimated 6.2 million refugees in Africa, but it's mostly Asian Middle Eastern refugees who find themselves in a long-term limbo situation: they cannot return home, but they cannot settle down for good in the country they have fled to. The vast majority of them live in refugee camps and receive aid from international aid agencies.

SA MYINT SWE AND NAN KHIN WIN'S STORY: FROM MYANMAR (BURMA) TO AUSTRALIA

Sa Myint Swe is 40 and came to Australia in 1996 with the help of a local refugee support group in New South Wales. He was joined by his wife Nan Khin Win and their newborn daughter Jasmine eight months later. Sa Myint Swe arrived on a permanent resident refugee visa. The only English he knew was "thank you."

"We left behind our families, our traditions, all that was familiar to us. We never thought that we would get out of that nightmare situation. Everywhere on the Thai-Burmese border we refugees were suffering—malaria and sickness, not enough food, no secure place to live, and constantly afraid of violence. You could easily get arrested by the corrupt Thai police and returned over the border to the Burmese military to be killed. Our dream for the future is that one day there will be democracy in Burma, and we will be able to go back."

In Australia, Sa Myint Swe went to daytime English classes and worked night shifts at a local Vietnamese bakery. Today, he and his wife own their own home and run a very popular Thai restaurant.

A new start

Every year, at least 20,000 refugees around the world are resettled through these programs. They offer refugees—who otherwise would probably remain in camps for the rest of their lives—the chance of a more secure and better existence. When the refugees arrive in their new country, they usually receive special help from the host government with language classes, finding a home, sending their children to school, and finding work.

A poster in a resettlement center welcomes refugees to New Zealand.

Sa Myint Swe, Nan Khin Win, and their daughter Jasmine.

33

Dangerous journeys

Basi is a Somali boy who fled from Somalia in a boat in the mid-1990s to escape the civil war in his country.

"We left by boat, but the boat broke down in the middle of the sea between Somalia and Kenya. One of our family fell in the water and drowned; it was our cousin. The boat finally reached the sand on a small island. There was nobody there, and for one day we slept on the sand. Some people came to collect us, and they took us to their island. We stayed there for a week. Then I was told that our family sent a small boat from Mombassa (Kenya) to that small island, and they took us, and we got to Kenya."

Basi and his family stayed in a refugee camp before they finally got to Europe.

These Cambodian asylum seekers were rescued by the Australian navy from the sinking boat in which they were traveling. They were held in a dentention center while their case was decided.

Smuggling increases

Today, the majority of asylum seekers are smuggled into the developed world. This is because they are usually unable to get documents to travel legally, and with greater restrictions on immigration and greater fears of terrorism, authorities around the world have increased documentation checks at ports and airports. Traveling without documentation has become all but impossible.

Smuggling routes

Asylum seekers often share the same smuggling routes with other migrants going abroad illegally to find work. Smuggling routes into western Europe, for example, can involve month-long journeys through several countries. People from Central American countries take weeks to reach the U.S. border and are at constant risk of being caught by the authorities at any border point.

Dangers of smuggling

As Western countries constantly tighten border controls and checks at ports and airports, smugglers often hide illegal migrants in the back of freight trucks, where they have to stay for days, often without enough water and food, until they get to a Western destination. Sea routes are also dangerous, particularly as the boats used are often small and poorly maintained.

A TRAGIC STORY: BEING SMUGGLED TO DEATH

In 2003, smugglers crammed around 70 illegal immigrants into the back of a refrigerator truck to take them from the U.S.-Mexican border to Houston. They had all paid to be smuggled into the U.S. In the course of the journey, 18 people died from lack of oxygen.

Survivors told officals that during the four-hour-long journey they had all been pounding on the walls and yelling to be let out. One of them phoned the emergency services from his mobile phone saying:

"We are in distress, we are in a trailer, we are asphyxiating."

But he could not tell them where they were.

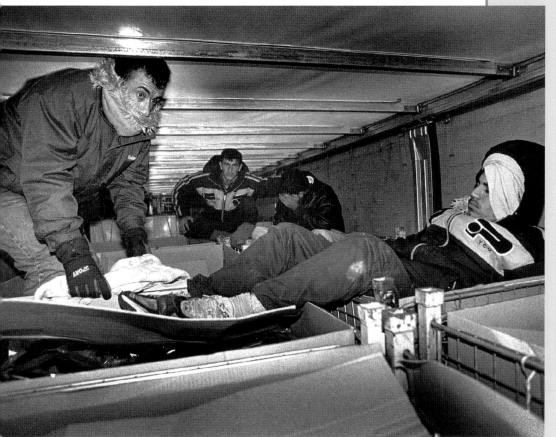

These illegal migrants have been found in a truck, where they were hidden by smugglers. Sadly, these makeshift hiding places can be death traps.

Staying for good

Applying to settle

In the era of mass immigration during the 19th and early 20th centuries, people did not get permission to move to the U.S. Even so, they went in the hope of being able to build a new life—and they usually did. Today, it is more difficult to go and live in another country for good. Countries such as Britain, Australia, New Zealand, Canada, and the U.S. offer only a limited legal opportunity for foreigners to settle. Each year, the governments of these countries decide on how many immigrants they want to accept.

Adding up the points

Prospective immigrants have to meet certain criteria before they can settle in these countries. They have to prove that they speak good English and that they have qualifications and skills in a profession that is useful to the host nation. They also have to show that they have enough savings that they will not have to rely on welfare support in the new country.

SELENA'S STORY: A CAREER IN A DIFFERENT CULTURE

Selena was 27 when she left her native Queensland, Australia, to experience Europe. She originally arrived on a 12-month working-vacation visa, but now has a highly skilled migrant visa allowing her to work and stay in Britain.

"I knew that as an accountant, I would always be able to secure employment abroad, and I wanted to experience a different environment. I came at a time when the economy was very good, and I had four job offers within days of my arrival in London. My prospects here are so much better, and there is so much culture and history to explore—I have no plans of returning to Australia just yet."

Many governments want to attract immigrants who bring with them desirable skills, such as computer expertise.

36

Change of lifestyle

Modern immigrants come from developed countries, too. Australia and New Zealand, for example, are particularly attractive to Europeans. At the start of the 21st century, British people were among Australia's top five immigrant nationality groups. Pull factors to these countries are often a warmer climate, a more "outdoors" lifestyle, the prospect of better housing, and, for children, better schooling.

THE PEARSE FAMILY'S STORY: LEAVING FOR THE GOOD LIFE

Simon and Chrissie Pearse and their two sons Zac and Wes entered a competition to live in Napier, New Zealand, for six months for free. Instead of living in a busy town in England, they now enjoy living by the sea surrounded by far fewer people.

"We used to be just focused on work, the boys, their soccer, and our regular summer [vacation] abroad. Here, life is such an adventure. Every weekend there is something different happening; we never know what we might be doing."

After the six months, they decided to stay in New Zealand for good. They have recently bought a new home, and Simon has found a permanent job in an engineering firm.

The Pearse family enjoying their new life in New Zealand.

Constant change

Colonial legacy

Migration patterns change all the time. In the past, migration flows were based on where colonial powers had set up colonies overseas. France, for example, used to rule Algeria and has received Algerian immigrants for a long time. Britain continues to receive large numbers of immigrants from Commonwealth countries, such as India and Sri Lanka, which used to be part of the British Empire.

A French McDonald's recognizes its Algerian Muslim community by wishing them a good Ramadan.

A TAMIL'S STORY: FROM SRI LANKA TO BRITAIN

During the 1980s and 1990s, many Sri Lankan Tamils fled the civil war in Sri Lanka (some Tamils wanted an independent Tamil state). Most came to Britain, as Sri Lanka is a former British colony. This Tamil refugee did not want to be named:

"I left because of the political problems. In 1986, when I was there in Jaffna, near my house there was the Tier movement [part of the Tamil separatist group], so the Sri Lankan army started bombing. We couldn't stay there. I wrote a letter to my sister in Britain, she wrote a sponsor letter to me, and I got a visa for three months. So I came with my children, and I asked for asylum at the airport."

Decision making

Today, the main factors affecting a migrant's decision where to go are the availability of work and how easy it is to get into the country. If countries close to home offer opportunities, people go there first. At least a million Ecuadorians, for example, live in the U.S., having left economic hardship in their country in the 1970s and 1980s. However, getting a visa into the U.S. is now very difficult, so many Ecuadorians have left for Europe instead. Spain's largest immigrant community is the Ecuadorians. This is because, until recently, travel to Spain from Ecuador was cheap and easy. The fact that Ecuadorians speak Spanish also made Spain more attractive to them than other European countries.

MAGDALENA'S STORY: PURSUING A DREAM

Magdalena is divorced with three children. In 1999, she wanted to leave Ecuador for the U.S., a place she dreamed about and where her movie star idol Arnold Schwarzenegger, also an immigrant, had made it big. But getting a visa to the U.S. proved impossible.

"My ideal was to go to California, for the beautiful landscape, what I've seen on television. But I knew it was a hard thing to accomplish."

But a friend suggested Magdalena come to Spain:

"She told me I could count on her. She sent me the ticket and the money they asked me to show at the airport to enter the country as a visitor. They didn't ask for a visa; it was very easy."

Language factor

Language does influence migrants' choices. Spain and Portugal, for example, now have a 400,000-strong Latin American immigrant community. But the most attractive destination countries continue to be those where English is spoken—such as the U.S., Britain, and Canada. For migrants with little or no skills, there is a wide availability of work in these countries. They are an attractive choice for educated migrants, too, because learning English will help their careers.

These children in China are learning English. English is taught as a second language in many schools around the world.

Friends and family

Migrants are increasingly prepared to travel longer distances if neighboring countries do not offer suitable work opportunities. Where possible, however, migrants rely on family members or friends to help them with information or contacts about jobs. Aneta probably would not have gone to Ireland had it not been for her friend.

A refugee steps off a bus. He will find life much easier if he has friends or family in his new home country.

Pushed and pulled

While migrants in the past had little idea what to expect in their new countries, migrants today know far more. The telephone, radio, television, and the Internet mean that people can find out a lot more about their destination countries before they go—and about what they can achieve there. The economic and political situations of many developing countries still push many migrants abroad in search of work, but information about the rest of the world often acts as a powerful pull factor, too.

Migration in perspective

It is, however, important to remember that the majority of people in the world remain in the country where they were born. Only about three percent of the world's population lives in a different country than the one in which they were born. Despite this low percentage, there are still millions of people migrating every year, but most of them move from one developing country to another. The developing world not only sends out the greatest number of migrants and immigrants, but it also receives them.

Globalization means that migrants are now much better informed about their destination countries.

Glossary

asylum Special legal immigration status given to people who are recognized as refugees according to the 1951 Convention on Refugees.

asylum seeker A person seeking asylum in another country because he or she fears persecution or danger in his or her own country.

Australasia The islands of the Southern Pacific Ocean, including Australia, New Zealand, and New Guinea.

British Empire The territories controlled by Britain from the 17th to mid-20th centuries as it expanded trade and conquered new lands. At its height, the British Empire covered almost 40 percent of the world's land.

cash crop Crop farmed purely for profit, not to be consumed by the farmer.

civil war Different groups fighting against each other in their own country.

colony Usually refers to an area of land controlled by a state that is overseas or abroad from it.

developed countries High-income countries where people have a high standard of living. These are usually found in Europe and North America, but also include Australia, New Zealand, and Japan.

developing countries Low- and middle-income countries where people have a lower standard of living and not as many goods and services available to them as in developed countries.

economic growth When the production of goods and services increases, more profit is being made and more and better paying jobs are created.

emigrant A person leaving his or her home country to live permanently in another country.

42

entrepreneur A person setting up a business.

European Union The union of 25 European countries which works toward shared economic and social goals.

green card An identity document that entitles a non-U.S. citizen to live and work in the U.S.

guest worker A person allowed to work in another country for a limited period only as a result of an agreement between the worker's home country and where he or she is working.

human rights Set of rights that everyone in the world should be entitled to, such as the right to free speech, the right to basic education, and the right to move freely to other countries.

hunter-gatherers Describes people who survive by hunting animals and gathering wild fruit and other food stuffs. Pre-historic people were nomadic hunter-gatherers.

immigrant A person who has moved permanently to another country to live and work.

immigration laws Laws that set out the circumstances under which people can live and work in a country not their own.

informal economy Businesses, usually on a small, local scale, that operate outside a country's formal tax and business regulations.

infrastructure Systems and facilities around which a country operates on a day-to-day basis, such as roads, banks, hospitals, water, and power supplies.

migrant A person going to work in another country, usually only for a limited time.

persecution Being punished, tortured, or mistreated by a government or a military group, usually because of one's political or religious beliefs or ethnic backround.

refugee A person who is recognized as a refugee under international law and is not able to return home for fear of his or her life or freedom.

refugee camp A settlement, usually temporary, that develops when people flee their homes during times of war or famine to go to a safer area near the borders of their own country.

resettlement program A special international program that allows refugees living in camps in developing countries to apply to live in a developed country.

smuggler A person helping another person to travel illegally into another country.

social status A person's standing in society, usually in terms of his or her occupation and wealth.

Soviet Union The first communist state, lasting from 1922 until 1991 and occupying modern day Russia and other, now independent, eastern European and Central Asian countries.

trafficker A person who smuggles people abroad and then forces them to work for him or her against their will.

United Nations An international organization bringing together representatives from 191 countries. The United Nations was set up in 1945 after World War II to uphold peace through international cooperation.

visa Official permission from a foreign country to visit it. This is usually given by the country's embassy, which puts a stamp in a person's passport to show that a visa has been granted.

World War II The biggest world conflict in history, involving most of the world's countries, fought from 1939 until 1945.

Web connections

International organizations
International Organization for Migration (IOM)
www.iom.int

International Labor Organization (ILO)
www.ilo.org

United Nations (UN)
www.un.org

United Nations High Commissioner for Refugees (UNHCR)
www.unhcr.ch

Nongovernmental organizations
Anti-Slavery International
www.antislavery.org
Campaigns against slavery and forced labor.

Australian Refugee Council
www.refugeecouncil.org.au
Supports asylum seekers and refugees in Australia.

British Refugee Council
www.refugeecouncil.org.uk
Supports asylum seekers and refugees in Britain.

Electronic Immigration Network
www.ein.org.uk
On-line gateway to resources on immigration and asylum worldwide.

National Immigration Forum
www.immigrationforum.org
Works to promote the rights of immigrants and refugees in the U.S.

U.S. Committee for Refugees
www.refugees.org
U.S. refugee charity.

Government sites
Australian Department of Immigration and Multicultural and Indigenous Affairs
www.immi.gov.au

UK Home Office Immigration and Nationality Directorate
www.ind.homeoffice.gov.uk

U.S. Citizenship and Immigration Services
www.uscis.gov/graphics/index.htm

Index